SWAMI VIVEKANANDA

Table of Contents

Arise! Awake and march forward;
stop not until you reach your destination.
Give me a few men and women who are pure
and unselfish and I shall shake the world.

The older I grow, the more everything seems to me to liein manliness. This is my new gospel.

American women! A hundred lives would not be sufficient to pay my deep debt of gratitude to you…

India is immortal, if she persists in her search for God.

Sisters and brothers of America!

—SWAMI VIVEKANANDA

HIS TEACHINGS TO ALL
SWAMI VIVEKANANDA

Ram Nivas Kumar

MA (English), MLISc., MJMC, Dip-in-OA

Edition

2024

Copyright
Ram Nivas Kumar

PREFACE

The Indian youth are at the crossroads. On the one hand, they see the pompous show of wealth and luxury; on the other, they see millions of people without enough food, clothes and shelter. India's invaluable spiritual heritage is in danger at the hands of materialistic thoughts.

At this critical juncture, the life, achievements and teachings of Swami Vivekananda can be of great importance to the nation and the youth. They contain India's spiritual treasure as against modern materialistic approach. His teachings are meant for people belonging to all strata of society of all religions and races.

This book is dedicated to the youth of India in high spirit. It has been written in a simple language and conversational style so that even a general reader of English may understand it easily.

While writing this book, Iwent through dozens of books on and by Swami Vivekananda. I went through the nine Volumes of "*The Complete Works Of Swami Vivekananda.*"I also contacted several scholars, academicians and educationists, the chief one being Swami Bhawatmananda, the Head of the Ramakrishna Mission Trust, Muzaffarpur, Bihar, whose blessings came me to the fore. I especially contacted an eminent scholar Dr. (Prof.) Satyendra Kumar, Ex-Head of the Department of English, S. N. Sinha College, Jehanabad, Bihar, presently working as a Senior Correspondent, United News of India, who went through the entire manuscript of this book and edited at large. I pay my high gratitude toboth of them.

While publishing this book, we have taken utmost care about accuracy of contents and other aspects. However, to err is human. Inadvertent errors, if any, may please be brought to our notice. Comments and suggestions are most welcome.

Hope, the youth, especially the students, will find this book as a treasure of nationalismand follow the footprints of His Highness Swami Vivekananda at high pitch. —***Ram Nivas Kumar***

WORDS OF EXPRESSION

Shri Ram Nivas Kumar is a sincere and dedicated official working at All India Radio, Patna. He is a rising star in the sky of English literature. He has written more than one dozen educational books. Almost all his books are dedicated to the students and the youth of India. Now, he has composed a book on the teachings of Swami Vivekananda which deserves full praise.

His present book is meant for the people belonging to all strata of society irrespective of caste or creed. The book has a wide range of teachings on almost all aspects of a civilized society. It is a perennial source of knowledge, especially for the students and the youth.

The author seems to have taken much pain in writing this book. He has covered a number of topics on manners and good behaviour that Swami Vivekananda delivered his teachings on. The book contains vivid knowledge on worldly affairs. It is inspirational for the whole world. The author depicts a true picture of an ideal society in his book.

I appreciate the thought and mind-set of the author. He is spreading the learning of Swami Vivekananda amongst the people living in India and abroad. Shri Kumar has performed a commendable job by presenting this book. His noble endeavours are highly appreciable.

I bless him to bloom in every sphere of life and pray the Almighty to shower upon him His best blessings.

Ved Prakash

Deputy Director General (E)

All India Radio, Patna

CONTENTS

1

SWAMI VIVEKANANDA
A ROLE MODEL OF INDIAN YOUTH

Swami Vivekananda was a great Hindu monk and religious philosopher. He possessed a manifold personality. He was a monk, teacher, mystic, philosopher, patriot and a saint—-all together. He had a leonine beauty matched with his great courage. He had respect for ancient religious traditions and beliefs. He had an immense knowledge of Eastern and Western cultures and a deep spiritual insight, eloquence and human sympathy.

He was born on 12th January, 1863. His childhood name was Narendranath Dutta. His father Shri Vishwanath Dutta was a well-known lawyer of Calcutta and mother Smt. Bhubneswari Devi, a very intelligent and pious lady.

His father Vishwanath often had scholarly discussions with his clients on world religion and Narendranath often used to join their discussions and express his views on the topics. Naren often used to say: "Point out where I'm wrong. If not, why should you object to my independent thinking?"

His mother was a great religious lady. She often taught Naren teachings of ethics and Puranas. Naren had deep interest in religious matters.

Narendranath was all-rounder. He could sing; was good at sports. He took much interest in wrestling, swimming and boxing. In addition to this, he was very fond of music. He was expert in playing on the tabla. He was a man of learning appetite. He often used to say that one should not ignore any art. Rather, one should always try to learn it. He gave much stress on physical strength as well as on mental one. He had a ready wit. His range of knowledge was immeasurable. He had a rational frame of mind. He loved to help people. He was a natural leader. Whatever he said during his speech, he first implemented it on himself. He was much sought-after by people.

Naren passed his BA (Philosophy) from General Assembly's Institution (now Scottish Church College) at Calcutta. As a student of Philosophy, the question of God and Its existence haunted his mind. Was there any God? If there was, what was He alike? What were men's relations with Him? Did He create this world which was so full of anomalies? He discussed these questions with many, but no one could give him satisfactory answer. He began to search persons who could say that they had seen God, but found none.

Someone had advised Narendranath to visit Ramakrishna at Dakshineswar who, he said, would be able to remove all his doubts about religion. As the days passed, Naren began to grow restless about the various riddles related to religion. He wanted to meet a man who could talk about God with authority of personal experience. Finally, he went to Ramakrishna one day and asked him straightway, if he had seen God. He (Ramakrishna) said, "He had and he could even show God to him. This naturally took Naren by surprise. Naren began to watch him from close quarters and after a long time he was left in no doubt that Ramakrishna was an extraordinary man. He was the only man he had so far met who had completely mastered himself. Naren loved and admired Ramakrishna but he never surrounded his independence of judgment. Interestingly, Ramakrishna himself did not demand it of him. Nevertheless, Naren gradually came to accept Ramakrishna his master. Ramakrishna wanted him to lead monastic life and hence gave him symbolically *Gerua* cloth. And then he assumed the name of Swami Vivekananda.

Swamiji was, first and foremost, a man of spirit, who had realized the ultimate truth. This was his most prominent facet of his multi-sided personality. Apart from this, he was a patriotic monk, quite out of the ordinary run off patriots; he was a social reformer of an unusual type; he was an educationist with several original plans and programmes; and he was blessed with a melodious voice which charmed his Master.

Swami Vivekananda travelled extensively throughout India. He was shocked to see the conditions of rural India—-people ignorant, superstitious, and half-starved and victims of caste tyranny. During the course of his travels, he met several members of intelligentsia—-lawyers, teachers, journalists and government officials. He appealed to all to do something for the masses. He began to deliver his learning like this:

Be pure. Live a clean life.

Defend your dignity and be respectful to others.

Be gentle and modest but do not hesitate to be firm when the situation requires.

Do not care else, if you are in the right.

Follow the truth always, whatever happens.

The body is dying every minute. The mind is constantly changing.

Freedom is only possible when no external power can exert any influence, produce any change.

Man is divine. Ye are the Children of God. Ye are the sharers of immortal bliss. Ye are holy and perfect beings.

Come up. O lions! Shake off the delusion that you are sheep. You are souls immortal. You are spirits free.

Everything that is strong, good and powerful in human nature is the outcome of divinity.

Manifest the divinity within you and everything will be harmoniously arranged around it.

We are what our thoughts have made us. So, take care of what you think. Words are secondary. Thoughts live, they travel afar.

Fill yourselves with the idea. Whatever you do, think well on it. All your actions will be magnified and transformed by the very power of the thought.

We must have friendship for all. We must be merciful towards those who are in misery. When people are happy, we ought to be happy.

Fight on bravely! Life is short! Give it up to a great cause.

Every step that has been really gained in the world has been gained by love. Criticism can never do any good. Condemnation accomplishes nothing.

Nothing makes us work so well at our best and highest as when all responsibility is thrown upon them.

Take the whole responsibility on your own shoulders. Know that you are the creator of your own destiny. All the strength you want is within yourselves. Therefore, make your own future. The infinite future is before you.

Inaction should be avoided by all means. Activity always means resistance. Resist all evils– mental and physical.

Even the greatest fool can accomplish a task, if it be after his heart. But the intelligent man is he who can convert every man into one that suits his taste. No work is petty.

Duty of any kind is not to be slighted. A man who does the lower work is not a lower man than a man who does the higher work.

A man should not be judged by the nature of his duties, but by the manner in which he does them.

Every duty is holy. And devotion to duty is the highest form of the worship of God.

You should work like a master and not as a slave. Work incessantly. Do not do slave's work.

No one can be altogether at rest. Ninety-nine per cent of mankind works like slaves and the result is misery. It is all selfish work. Work through freedom! Work through love!

Advance like a hero. Don't be thwarted by anything.

Imitation is not civilization. Imitation never makes for progress.

Be brave. Whenever darkness comes, assert the reality. Mountain-high though the difficulties appear, terrible and gloomy though all things seem, they are but delusions. Fear not. It will banish. Crush it and it vanishes. Stamp upon it and it dies. Be not afraid. Think not how many times you fail. Never mind. Time is infinite. Go onward and light must come.

Go on bravery. Do not expect success in a day or two. Always hold on to the highest. Be steady. Avoid jealousy and selfishness. Be obedient and eternally faithful to the cause of truth, humanity and your country and you will move the world.

Men are more valuable than all the wealth of the world.

My brave boys! Nothing else is necessary but these- love, sincerity, and patience.

Help the poor; feed the poor. Give them food to eat and water to drink. Serve them as much as you can. I guarantee; you will get peace.

There is nothing insurmountable in this world. Only condition is—one must get association of able and right persons.

A teacher can be a true guide and philosopher, if he takes his job sincerely. And if he performs it honestly, even mountains can give safe passage.

A pupil must have unflinching faith in his teacher.

The only religion in the world is the religion of universal love. The sooner it is understood, the better it would be for a man and the nation.

Whenever stress and strain envelop a person, he should look into his mind and try to understand the situation and devise ways to come out of it.

One should not form an opinion which is too staunch and unchangeable. One must be ready to undergo change and accept and adopt what is right and correct. Dogmatic attitude can never help.

Every soul is potentially divine. The goal is to manifest this divinity within by controlling nature—external and internal. Dothis either by work or worship.

Everything that is strong and good and powerful in human nature is the outcome of that divinity.

Man stands on the glory of his own soul, the infinite, the eternal,the deathless—that soul which no instruments can pierce, which no air can dry, no fire burn, no water melt, the infinite, the birthless, the deathless without beginning and without end... This glorious soul we must believe in. Out of that will come power.

The germ of infinite perfection exists in all. We should cultivate the optimistic temperament, and endeavour to see the good that dwells in everything.

You must know what you are, what your real nature is. You must become conscious of that infinite nature within. Then your bondage will burst.

Think all of you that you are the infinitely powerful Atman, and see what strength comes out.

Every religion and every creed recognizes man as divine.

There are three things in the make-up of man. There is the body, there is the mind, and there is the soul.

My faith is in younger generation, the modern generation, out of them will come my workers. They will work out the whole problem, like lions.

2

TEACHINGS OF SWAMI VIVEKANANDA

Teachings of Swami Vivekananda in a nutshell are enumerated below for ready reference to the students:

Destroy nothing: Don't destroy. Break not. Pull not anything down. Help others, if you can. If not, fold your hands. Don't injure if you cannot render them any help.

Salutations to the working masses: Be unselfish. Have devotion to duty. Have interest even in the smallest act. Swami Vivekananda had deep love for working masses. He taught us to act as he did.

The great national sin: To neglect the masses is the cause of our downfall. No amount of politics would be of any avail until the mass in India are well-educated, well-fed and well-cared for. If we want to regenerate India, we must work for them.

Religion is not to blame: Religion is not in fault. Your religion teaches you that every being is only your own self multiplied. Follow the great teachings of the Hindu faith. Hindu religion is the mother of all religions. Society exists on account of religion.

Know your past: Look back out of the very past of your motherland. Drink deep the eternal fountain. March forward and make India brighter, greater and much higher than she ever was. Your ancestors were great. We must first read them.

Deluge the land with spiritual ideas: Keep the motto before you- "Elevation of the masses without injuring their religion." In religion lies the vitality of Indians. If you throw off your religion, you will become extinct. Work through the vitality of your religion. India requires first of all an upheaval in religion. So, first deluge the land with spiritual ideas. The Indian mind is first religious, then anything else.

Not by religion alone: We need first bread; then religion. Material civilization is necessary to create work for the poor. India is to be raised.

The poor are to be fed. Education is to be spread. And the evil of priest craft is to be removed.

Working of womanhood: The uplift of women is a prime factor. Awakening of the masses must come first. All nations have attained greatness by paying proper respect to woman. The country and the nation which do not respect women have never become great; nor will ever be in future.

The urgent need for education: The only service to be done to our lower classes is to give them education. To develop the individuality of the masses, they are to be given idea. Their eyes are to be opened to what is going in the world ground and then they will work out their own salvation. Every nation; every man and every woman must work out their own salvation. Give them ideas. That is the only help they require. Our duty is to put ideas into their heads. And they will do the rest. This is what is to be done in India. Even for society, the first duty is to educate the people, and you will have to wait till that time comes.

Self-help: All the wealth of the world cannot help one little Indian village, if the people are not taught to keep themselves. Our work should be mainly educational—-both moral and intellectual.

Reciprocity between the East and the West: SwamiJi says: For a complete civilization the world is waiting; waiting for the treasures to come out of India. The world is waiting for India's marvelous spiritual inheritance. Therefore, we must go out. Exchange our spirituality for anything they have to give us.

Give and take is the law. If India wants to raise herself, she must bring out her treasures and throw them among the nations of the earth and in turn be ready to receive what others have to give her. Expansion is life; contraction is death. Love is life and hatred is death. We commenced to die the day we began to hate other races. We must mix with all the races of the earth.

Therefore, we must go out; exchange our spirituality for anything.We will not be students always, but teachers also. There cannot be friendship without equality. And there cannot be equality when one party is always the teacher and the other party sits always at his feet. If you want to become equal with the Englishman or the American, you will have to teach as well as learn.

India has to learn from Europe the conquest of external nature and Europe has to learn from India the conquest of internal nature. Then, there will be neither Hindus nor Europeans. There will be the ideal humanity.

Indian has to be built upon Indian tradition. We must grow according to our nature. We should not adopt foreign line of tradition. What is meant for others may be poisonous. So, we should allow our own bent run in our own grooves.

Be patient. Love the race. It has done great things for us in the past. Love, sincerity and patience are necessary for the uplift of our nation. Love is life. It is the only love of life. Selfishness is death. And this is true here,there and everywhere.

The Hindus have received their religion through revelation- the Vedas. They hold that the Vedas are without beginning and without end. Vedas are not mere books. They are the accumulated treasury of spiritual laws. It is the laws that govern the spiritual world. The moral, ethical, and spiritual relations between soul and soul, and between individual spirit and the Father of all spirits, were there before their discovery, and would remain even if we forgot them.

The discoverers of these laws are called Rishis, and we honour them as perfect beings. The Vedas teach us that creation is without beginning and without end. Science is said to have proved that the sum total of cosmic energy is always the same. Then, if there was all this manifested energy! Some say it was in a potential form in God. In that case, God is sometimes potential and sometimeskinetic, which would make Him mutable. Everything mutable is a compound, and everything compound must undergo that change which is called destruction. So God would die, which is absurd. Therefore, there never was a time when there was no creation.

Creation and Creator are two lines, without beginning and without end, running parallel to each other.God is the ever active providence, by whose power systems after systems are being evolved out of chaos, made to run for a time and again destroyed. This is what the Brahmin boy repeats everyday: The sun and the moon, the Lord created like the suns and moons of previous cycles. And this agrees with modern science.

The Vedas declare, I am a spirit living in a body. I am notthe body. The body will die, but I shall not die Here am I in this body; it will fall, but I shall go on living. I had also a past. The soulwas not created, for creation means a combination which means a certain future dissolution.

Vivekananda on Science: Science is nothing but the finding of unity. As soon as science would reach perfect unity, it would stop making further progress, because it would reach the goal. Thus chemistry could not progress farther when it would discover one element out of which all other would be made. Physics would stop when it would be able to fulfill its services in discovering on energy of which all others are but manifestations,and the science of religionbecomes perfect when it would discover Him who is the only one in the Universe of death, Himwho is the constant basis of an ever-changing world. One who is the only soul of which all souls are but delusivemanifestation.Religion can go no farther. This is the goal of all sciences.

Vivekananda on Religion: To the Hindu, the whole world of religion is only a travelling, a coming up of different men and women, through various conditions and circumstances to the same goal. Every religion is the material man, and the same Goal is the inspirer of all of them.

The Lord had declared to the Hindu in His incarnation as Krishna, "I am in every religion as the thread through a string of pearls. Wherever thou seest extraordinary holiness and extraordinary power raising and purifying humanity, know thou that I am there." I challenge the world to find throughout the whole system of Sanskrit philosophy, and such expression on that the Hindu alone will be saved and not others. Says Vyasa: We find perfect men even beyond the pale of our caste and creed. Then how can the Hindu, whose whole fabric of thought centres in Lord, believe the Buddhism which is agnostic, or in Jainism which is atheistic.

The Buddhists and the Jains do not depend upon God, but the whole force of their religion is directed to the great central truth in every religion- to evolve God out of man.

May He who is the Brahman of the Hindus, the Ahura-Mazda of the Zoroastrians, the Buddha as the Buddhist, the Jehovah of the Jews, and the Father in the Heaven of the Christians give strength to you to carry on your noble idea. The star arose in the east.

Swami Vivekananda says: Three things are necessary to make every man great; every nation great—-

I.Recognition of the powers of goodness.

II.Absence of jealousy and suspicion.

III.Helping all who are trying to be good and do better.

Do not be afraid of a small beginning. Great things come afterwards.

Be courageous. Do not try to lead your brethren, but serve them. The brutal mania for leading has sunk many a great ship in the waters of life. Be unselfish even unto death and work without any partiality.

Have faith that you are all. You are born to do great things. Let not the barks of puppies frighten you. No. Not even the thunderbolt from the sky. Just stand up and work.

We want men; men of the mind and muscle. It is man that makes everything. Men are more valuable than all the wealth of the world.

Whatever others think or do, lower not our standard of purity, morality and love for God. One who loves God need not fear any jugglery. Holiness is the highest divine power on the earth and in the heaven.

Trust not the so called rich. They are more dead than alive. The hope lies in you– in the meek, the lowly but the faithful. Forward onward!

Do not look up to the so-called rich and greedy. Do not care for the heartless intellectual writers and their cold-blooded newspapers' articles.

Our glory lies in the Lord. So, march on! LORD is our General. Do not look back to who fails. Forward onward! One falls, and another takes up the work.

The use of higher education is to find out how to solve the problems of life. Higher education does not mean mere study of material sciences and turning out things of everyday use by machinery. (The Complete Works of Swami Vivekananda, Vol-V, p-368)

There should be an institution to train teachers who must go about preaching religion and giving secular education to our people. (Vol-III, p-303)

It would be better if people get a technical education so that they might find work and even their bread instead of dawdling about and trying for service. (Vol-V, p-367)

What we need is to study, independent of foreign control, different branches of the knowledge that is our own. We may read books, hear lectures, and talk miles, but experience is the one teacher, the one eye-opener. We learn through smiles and tears.Practice is absolutely necessary. If you do not practise, you will not get one step further. It all depends on practice. (Vol-I, p-139)

All our knowledge is based upon experience. It is practice first and knowledge afterwards. (Vol-II, p-317)

The greatness of the teacher consists in the simplicity of his language. Simplicity is the secret to success. Every man is capable of receiving knowledge if it is imparted in his own language. The language in which we naturally express ourselves, in which we communicate our anger, grief, or love, etc.—-there cannot be a fitter language than that. (Vol-VI, p-187)

Go and preach to all, "Arise, awake, sleep no more; within each of you there is the power to remove all wants and all miseries. Believe this, and that power will be manifested." (Vol-VI, p-454)

All the great personages from Buddha down to Chaitanya and Ramakrishna, who came for the well-being of the world, taught the common people in the languages of the people themselves. (Vol-VI, p-187)

Bring out the gems of spirituality that are stored up in our books and in the possession of a few only. The idea must be taught in the language of the people at the same time. Sanskrit education must go allalong with it, because the very word sound of Sanskrit words give a practice and a power and strength to the race.

Sanskrit is the language of God. It is a divine language. Sanskrit and prestige go together in India. In Philology, our Sanskrit language is now universally acknowledged to be the foundation of all European languages, which, in fact, are nothing but jargonized Sanskrit. (Vol-III, p-299)

If there is inequality in nature, there must be equal chance for all—or if greater for some and for some less—the weaker should be given more chances than the stronger. In other words, greater help must be given to him whom nature has not endowed with an acute intellect from birth. All the members of society ought to have the same opportunity for obtaining wealth, education, or knowledge.

Women have many grave problems. *Brahmacharinis* of education and character should take up the task of teaching. (Vol-V, p-231)

In villages and towns, they will open centres and strive for the spread of female education through such devout preachers of characters. Then, there will be the real spread of female education in the country.

History and the Puranas, house-keeping and the arts, the duties of home life and principlesthat make for the development of an ideal character have to be taught. (Vol-VI, p-89)

Other matters such as sewing culinary art, rules of domestic workand upbringing of children will also be taught while *Japa*,worship and meditation shall form an indispensable part of the teaching.

Along with the other things they should acquire the spirit of valour and heroism. In the present day, it has become necessary for them also to learn self-defense. (Vol-V, p-342)

Religion, arts, science, house-keeping, cooking, sewing, hygiene-the simple essential points in these subjects ought to be taught to our women. (Vol-VI, p-493-494)

Women must be put in a position to solve their own problems in their own ways. And our Indian women are as capable of doing it as any in the world. (Vol-V, p-229-230)

It is only in the homes of educated and pious mothers that great men are born. The uplift of women and the awakening of the masses must come out and then only can any real good come out for the country, for India. (Vol-VI, p-489-490)

Never lose faith in yourself;you can do anything in this universe. Never weaken, all power is yours. (Vol-VII, p-85)

It is the coward and the fool who say, "This is fate." But it is the strong man who stands up and says, "I will make my fate." (Vol-VIII, p-184)

If what we are now has been the result of our own past actions, it certainly follows that whatever we wish to be in future can be produced by our present actions. So, we have to know how to act——by knowing how to work,one can obtain the greatest results——even the lowest forms of work are not to be despised. (Vol-I, p-31)

Feel that you are great andyou become great...We all have the same glorious soul, let us believe in it. (Vol-III, p-243)

Have faith in yourselves, great convictions are the mothers of great deeds. (Vol-V, p-30)

Losing faith in one's self means losing faith in God. (Vol-III, p-376)

Infinite faith and strength are the only conditions of success. (Vol-V, p-78)

Every boy should be trained to practice absolute *Brahmacharya*, and then faith—-Shraddah will come. (Vol-V, p-369)

Be possessed of Shraddah (faith), of Virya (courage), attain to the knowledge of the Atman, and sacrifice your life for the good of others—this is my wish and blessing. (Vol-VII, p-267)

Sincerity of conviction and purity of motive will surely gain the day. (Vol-IV, p-278)

3

TEACHINGS FROM THE COMPLETE WORKS OFSWAMI VIVEKANANDA

His teachings are further enumerated from different Volumes of "The Complete Works of Swami Vivekananda" for our students and the youth to read, understand and emulate for the cause of the nation:

You fail only when you do not strive sufficiently.

As soon as a man or a nation loses faith, death comes.

Have faith in yourself. And have faith in God. This is the secret of greatness. (The Complete Works of Swami Vivekananda) (Vol-III, p-190)

Never think—-there is anything impossible for soul. (Vol-II, p-308)

What you think, that you will be. If you think yourself weak, weak you will be. If you think yourself strong, strong you will be. (Vol-III, p-130)

Take your stand on good purpose, right means and righteous courage and be brave.

The world can be good and pure, only if our lives are good and pure. Therefore, let us purify ourselves. (Vol-VI, p-281)

Never mind the struggles, even if you fail a thousand times. (Vol-II, p-152)

This human body is the greatest body in the universe and human being is the greatest being. (Vol-I, p-142)

We are responsible for what we are. (Vol-I, p-31)

Be strong, my young friend!—-that is my advice to you. This is the great fact- strength is life; weakness is death. (Vol-III, p-242)

Death is better than a vegetating ignorant life. It is better to die on the battle field than to die a life of defeat. (Vol-II, p-124)

Whatever you do, devote your whole mind, heart and soul to it. (The Life of Swami Vivekananda, p-284)

Ninety per cent of thought food is wasted by the ordinary human being. And, therefore, he is constantly committing blunders. This is the cause of misery. (Vol-VI, p-123-124)

No force can be created; it can only be directed. (Vol-VIII, p-46)

Arise! Awake and march forward; stop not until you reach your destination!

Never say—-'No.' Never say—-'I cannot'. You can do anything and everything. (Vol-II, p-300)

The road to the good is the roughest and steepest in the universe. Character is to be established through a thousand stumbles. (Vol-VIII, p-382)

Education is the manifestation of the perfection. To me, the very essence of education is the concentration of mind and not the collecting of facts. (Vol-IV, p-358)

Great work requires great and persistent efforts for a long time. (Vol-VIII, p-383)

Misery is caused by ignorance and nothing else. (Vol-VII, p-501)

We need to have three things—-the heart to feel, the brain to conceive and the hand to work. Make yourself a dynamo. Feel first for the world. (Vol-VI, p-144)

Great men are those who build highways for others with their heart's blood. (Vol-VI, p-273)

The difference between God and devil is in nothing except in unselfishness and selfishness. (Vol-I, p-425)

Virtue is that which tends to our improvement. Vice is that which tends to our degeneration. (Vol-VI, p-112)

Unselfishness is God. (Vol-I, p-87)

The secret of religion lies not in theories but in practice. To be good and do good is the whole of religion. (Vol-VI, p-245)

Religion is the manifestation of the natural strength that is in man. (Vol-VIII, p-185)

The basic aim of religion is to bring peace to man. One must be happy here and there. Any religion that can bring about is the true religion for humanity. (Reminiscence of Swami Vivekananda, p-45/46)

It is my firm conviction that no great work is accomplished in this world by the low cunning. (Vol-VII, p-125)

The world will crumble into dust if it does not make spirituality the basis for its life. And what will save Europe is the religion of the Upanishads. (Uttered by Swami Vivekananda in 1897 (Vol-III, p-159)

Be moral. Be brave. Be a heart-whole man. (Vol-V, p-3)

The debt which the world owes to our motherland is immense. (Vol-III, p-105)

India will be raised not with the power of the flesh, but with the power of the spirit. (Vol-IV, p-352)

A captain must sacrifice his head. If you can lay down your life for a good cause, then only you can be a leader. (Vol-VII, p-325)

Learn obedience first. Our spirit of independence and spirit of obedience should be equally strong. (Vol-VI, p-349)

No individual can leave by holding itself apart from the community of others. Give and take is the law. Expansion is life. Contraction is death. (Vol-IV, p-365)

A great national sin is the neglect of the masses. No amount of politics would be of any avail until the masses in India are well educated, wellfed, and well cared for. If we want to regenerate India, we must work for them. (Vol-V, p-222)

Make your nerves strong. What we want is muscles of iron and nerves of steel. (Vol-III, p-224)

Be unselfish. Never listen to one friend in private accusing another. (Vol-IV, p-369)

Better to die like heroes than to die as stocks and stones. Better to wear out than to rust out specially for the sake of doing the least good to others. (Vol-VII, p-176)

A handful of men can throw the world off its hinges, provided they are wanted in thought, work and deed. Never forget this conviction. (Vol-VII, p-372)

You must not depend on any foreign help. (Vol-V, p-109)

Work unto death. It is better to die on the field of duty than to die like a worldly worm. (Vol-V, p-114)

Doing well to others is virtue; injuring others is sin. Strength and manliness are virtue; weakness and cowardice are sin. Independence is virtue; dependence is sin. Loving others is virtue; hating others is sin. (Vol-V, p-419)

True equality has never been and can never be on the earth. (Vol-I, p-113)

Help comes from within you. (Vol-II, p-324)

Be free. Hope for nothing from anyone. (Vol-II, p-324)

If you fail a thousand times, make the attempt once more. (Vol-II, p-152)

The remedy for weakness is not brooding over weakness, but thinking of strength. (Vol-II, p-300)

To succeed, you must have tremendous perseverance and will-power. (Vol-I, p-178)

Come and do something heroic. (Vol-VI, p-314)

Be not in despair. The way is very difficult like walking on the edge of a razor. Yet, despair not.

Be your own self. Why weepiest thou, brother? There is neither death nor disease for thee. There is neither misery nor misfortune for thee. Thou are Existence Absolute... (Vol-V, p-275)

Let people say whatever they like. Stick to your conviction. The world will be at your feet. (Vol-VI, p-274)

Have faith in yourself first. All power is in you. Be conscious and bring it out. Say—"I can do everything." Even the poison of a snake is powerless if you can firmly deny it. (Vol-VI, p-274)

Face the terrible. Face it boldly. (Vol-I, p-338)

Stand up and fight. Fight it out whatever comes. Taking a step backward, you do not avoid any misfortune. It does not befit you to be a slave. So, Arise! Awake! Stand up and fight! (Vol-I, p-461)

This human body is the greatest body in the universe. And a human being is the greatest being. (Vol-I, p-142)

This world is the great gymnasium where we come to make ourselves strong. (Vol-V, p-410)

We reap what we sow. We are the makers of our own fate. (Vol-II, p-224)

Don't fly away from the wheels of the world-machine; but stand inside it and learn the secret of work. (Vol-I, p-115)

Purity, patience and perseverance are the three essentials to success. (VI-VI, p-281)

Every fool may become a hero at one time or another. (Vol-I, p-29)

Education is not the amount of information that is put to your brain and runs riot all your life. We must have life building, man-making and character making assimilation of ideas. (Vol-III, p-302)

Knowledge is inherent in man. No knowledge comes from outside. It is all inside. (Vol-I, p-28)

The external world is simply the suggestion which sets us to study our own mind. (Vol-I, p-28)

First learn to obey. The command will come by itself. Always first learn to be a servant, and then you will be fit to be a master. (Vol-III, p-134/135)

We want education by which character is formed, strength of mind is increased, the intellect is expanded and by which one can stand on one's own feet. (Vol-V, p-342)

Each nation has a mission for the world. So long as the mission is not hurt, the nation lives. As soon as its mission is hurt, the nation collapses. (Vol-VIII, p-74/75)

Selfishness is a sin. (Vol-III, p-143)

The good live for others. The wise man should sacrifice himself for others. (Vol-VI, p-317)

Do well to humanity and to the world of love. If death is so certain, it is better to die for a good cause. (Vol-VI, p-265)

This world is not for cowards. Do not try to fly. Look not for success or failure. Join yourself to the perfectly unselfish will and work on. (Vol-VI, p-83)

Live in the midst of the battle of life. (Vol-VI, p-84)

It is fear alone that is death. You have to go beyond all fear. So, from this day be fearless. (Vol-VI, p-473)

Religion is the idea which is raising the brute unto man, and man unto God. (Vol-V,p-409)

Man is an infinite circle whose circumference is nowhere but the centre is located in one spot. God is an infinite circle whose circumference is nowhere but whose centre is everywhere. (Vol-II, p-33)

The definition of morality is this: That which is selfish is immoral; and that which is unselfish is moral. (Vol-I, p-10)

Have faith that you are all born to do great things. Let not the barks of puppies frighten you, not even the thunderbolt from the sky. But stand and work. (Vol-V, p-43)

Utter no word of condemnation. Close your lips and let your heart open. Work out the salvation of this land and of the whole world. (Vol-III, p-199)

Have fire and spread all over. Be the servant while leading. Be unselfish. Never listen to one friend in private accusing another. (Vol-IV, p-369)

The history of the world is the history of persons like Buddha and Jesus. The passionless and unattached do most for the world. (Vol-VIII, p-226)

When there is a conflict between the heart and the brain, let the heart be followed. It is the heart which takes one to the highest place. (Vol-I, p-412)

He is an atheist who does not believe in himself. (Vol-II, p-311)

To succeed, you must have tremendous perseverance, tremendous will. (Vol-I, p-178)

You must have an iron will if you would have to cross the ocean. You must be strong enough to pierce mountains. (Vol-VI, p-297)

The whole world is in our own mind. Learn to see things in the proper light. (Vol-I, p-440)

Ours is not to reason why; ours is but to do and die. Be of good cheer and believe that we are selected by the Lord to do great things and we will do them. (Vol-V, p-23)

We can overcome the difficulty by constant practice. We must learn that nothing can happen to us unless we make ourselves susceptible to it. (Vol-II, p-7)

The highest things are under your feet, because you are Divine Stars. (Vol-VIII, p-186-187)

Each work has to pass through these stages—-ridicule, opposition, and then acceptance. Each man who thinks ahead of his time is sure to be misunderstood. So, opposition and persecution are welcome. Only I have to be steady and pure and must have immense faith in God. And all these will vanish. (Vol-V, p-91)

Let us all work hard, my Brethren! This is no time for sleep. On our work, depends the coming of the India of future. (Vol-III, p-154)

My faith is in younger generation; the modern generation. Out of them will come my workers.They will work out the whole problems. (Vol-V, p-223)

If you are really my children, you will fear nothing, stop at nothing. You will be like lions. You must rouse India and the whole world. My children must be ready to jump into fire, if needed. (Vol-V, p-61)

Go, all of you, wherever an outbreak of plague or famine is, or wherever the people are in distress, and mitigate their sufferings. At the most, you may die in the attempt. What of that, if death is so certain? (Vol-V, p-383)

Die you must but have a great ideal to die for. It is better to die with a great ideal in life. (Vol-V, p-383/384)

Let us all be honest. If we cannot follow the ideal, let us confess our weakness. (Vol-IV, p-145)

Let people praise you or blame you. Let fortune smile or frown upon you. Let your body fall today or after a *yuga*. See that you do not deviate from the path of truth. (Vol-VII, p-126)

My hope and faith rest in men like you. Understand my words in true spirit and apply yourselves to work. I have given you advice enough. Now, put at least something in practice. Let the world see that your listening to me has been a success. (Vol-VII, p-175)

You must learn to make the physique very strong and teach the same to others. Walk in the mornings and evenings and do physical labour. Body and mind must run parallel. It won't do to depend on others in everything. (Vol-VII, p-171)

There is only one method to attain knowledge and that is called concentration. (Vol-I, p-130)

The veryessence of education is the concentration of mind. (Vol-VI, p-38)

The main difference between men and animals is the difference in their power of concentration. An animal has very little power of concentration. All success in any line of work is the result of this.

The power of concentration is the only key to the treasure house of knowledge. How to check it and bring the mind under control is the whole subject of study in Raja-yoga. (Vol-II, p-391)

Practice of meditation leads to mental concentration. (Vol-VI, p-486)

To me, the very essence of education is the concentration of mind, not the collecting of facts. If I had to do my education over again and had any voice in the matter, I would not study facts at all. I would develop the power of concentration and detachment, and then with a perfect instrument I could collect the facts at will side by side, in the choice. (Vol-VI,p-38)

Education is not filling of mind with a lot of facts. Perfecting the instrument and getting complete mastery of my own mind is the ideal of education. If I want to celebrate my mind upon a point, it goes there. (Vol-I, p-510)

Power comes to him who observes unbroken *Brahmcharya* for a period of twelve years. (Vol-V, p-358)

Complete continence gives great intellectual and spiritual power. (Vol-VII, p-67)

Controlled desire leads to the highest result. Transform the sexual energy into spiritual energy. But do not emasculate, because that is throwing away the power. The stronger this force, the more can be done with it. Only a powerful current of water can do hydraulic mining.

By the observance of strict *Brahmcharya* (continence) all learning can be mastered in a very short time. It is owing to this want of continence that everything is on the brink of ruin. (Vol-VII, p-224)

Chastity of thought, word, and deed, always and in all conditions, is called *Brahmcharya*. (V-I, p-190)

Unchaste imagination is as bad as unchaste action. (Vol-VII, p-69)

Every word should be trained to practice absolute *Brahmcharya*, and then, and then only, faith (Sraddha)—will come. (Vol-V, p-369)

The *Brahmcharya* must be sexually pure in thought, word, and deed. (Vol-VII, p-67)

No one could obtain intellectual greatness until he was physically pure. Morality gave strength; the immoral were always weak, and could never raise themselves intellectually, much less spiritually. (Vol-IX, p-519)

In every man, there is more or less of this *Ojas* stored up. All the forces that are working in the body in their highest become *Ojas*. (Vol-I, p-169)

All the senses, external and internal, must be under the disciple's control. You should be able to say to your mind, "You are mine; I order you, do not see or hear anything." (Vol-VIII, p-110)

Never allow weakness to overtake your mind. (Vol-VII, p-234)

Physical weakness is the cause of one third of our miseries. (Vol-III, p-241)

All knowledge depends upon calmness of mind. (Vol-VII, p-72)

If you have to think, think good thoughts, great thoughts. (Vol-VIII, p-131)

Doing is very good, but that comes from thinking. Fill the brain, therefore, with high thoughts, highest ideals, place them day and night before you, and out of that will come great work. (Vol-II, p- 861)

We are what our thoughts have made us. So take care of what you think. (Vol-VII, p-14)

What we think, we become. (Vol-VIII, p-19)

Like fire in a piece of flint, knowledge exists in the mind; suggestion is the friction which brings it out. (Vol-I, p-28)

The whole world is in our minds. Learn to see things in proper light. (Vol-I, p-441)

Pleasure is not the goalof life, but knowledge is. (Vol-I, p-27)

Knowledge is the goal of all life. (Vol-IV, p-210)

The real life of man consists of knowledge. (Vol-1, p-52)

Instinct, reason, and inspiration are the three instruments of knowledge. (Vol-II, p-389)

The gift of knowledge is the highest gift in the world. (Vol-VII, p-256)

No action can give you freedom. Only knowledge can make you free. (Vol-VII, p-54)

Knowledge is irresistible; the mind cannot take it or reject it. When it comes, the mind has to accept it. So, it is not a work of the mind; only its expression comes in the mind. (Vol-VII, p-54)

Knowledge itself is the highest reward of knowledge.(Vol-I, p-130)

Knowledge alone can make us perfect. (Vol-VII, p-38)

When we hear beautiful music; our minds become fastened upon it.

He alone is the real great man whose character is great always. (Vol-I, p-29)

Your country requires heroes; be heroes! (Vol-V, p-51)

You must have strict morality. Deviate an inch from this, and you are gone forever. (Vol-VII, p-447)

Truthis purity, truth is all-knowledge, truth must be strong in, must be enlightening, must be invigorating. (Vol-III, p-225)

Truth does not pay homage to any society. Society has to pay homage to truth or die. Societies should be molded upon truth; and truth has not to adjust itself to society. (Vol-II, p-84)

That society is the greatest where the highest truth becomes practical. Thatis my opinion. And if society is not fit for the highest truths, make it so.(Vol-II, p-85)

Practice that boldness which knows the truth, which dares show the truth in life. (Vol-II, p-85)

Everything can be sacrificed for truth, but truth cannot be sacrificed for anything. (Vol-V, p-410)

Unselfishness is more paying. (Vol-I, p-32)

The unselfishness is the test of religion. He who has more of this unselfishness is more spiritual. (Vol-III, p-143)

Man thinks foolishly that he can make himself happy, and after years of strugglefinds out at last that true happiness consists in killing selfishness and that no one can make him happy except himself. (Vol-I, p-84)

This is the only sin—-to say that you are weak, or others are week. (Vol-II, p-308)

Infinite strength is religion and God.Avoid weakness and slavery. (Vol-VII, p-13)

Whether you believe in spirituality or nor; for the sake of the national life, you have to get tohold or spirituality and keep to it. Then, stretch the other hand out and gain all you can from other races. (Vol-III, p-153)

Religion is not in books, nor in theories; not in dogmas, nor in talking;not even in reasoning. It is being and becoming. (Vol-III, p-253)

I do not believe in God or religion which cannot wipe the widow's tears or bring a piece of bred to the orphan's mouth. (Vol-V, p-50)

Religion is the manifestation of the divinity already in man. (Vol-IV, p-358)

Religion is the manifestation of the natural strength that is in man. (Vol-VIII, p-185)

What we want are western science coupled with Vedanta, Brahmcharya, as the guiding motto, and also Shraddha and faith in one's own self. (Vol-V, p-366)

Say, "Everything is in me, and I can manifest it at will." (Vol-VI, p-277)

Cherish positive thoughts. By dwelling too much upon negativism, the whole country is going to ruin! (Vol-VI, p-273)

Struggle is the sign of life. (Vol-VII, p-219)

Perseverance will finally conquer. Nothing can be done in a day. (Vol-II, p-152)

The world sympathizes only with the strong and the powerful. (Vol-V, p-239)

Men should be taught to be practical and physically strong. A dozen of such lions will conquer the world, but not millions of sheep can do so. (Vol-V, p-315)

First build up your physique. Then only you can get control over the mind. (Vol-VII, p-155)

Brahmcharya should be like a burning fire within the veins. (Vol-IX, p-423)

Holiness is the greatest power. Everything else quails before it. (Vol-VI, p-89)

Out of purity and silence comes the word of power. (Vol-VII, p-16)

Superstition is a great enemy of man. (Vol-I, p-15)

What is done is done. Do not repent. Do not brood over past deeds.

On you lie the future hopes of our country. I feel extreme pain to see you leading a life of inaction. Set yourselves to work.

Work! Do not tarry.Do not sit idle, thinking that everything will be done in time, later on! Mind you... Nothing will be done that way! (Vol-V, p-384)

Idleness won't do. Throwoverboard all idea of jealousy and egotism once for all. Come on to the practical field with tremendous energy to workin the fullness of strength! (Vol-VI, p-265)

That you may catch my fire, that you may be intensely sincere, that you die the heroes' death on the field of battle—-is the constant prayer of Vivekananda. (Vol-V, p-66)

INDIA'SFUTURE: Shall India die? No. Not, never. India is made up of spirituality, ideality and moral perfection. She has sympathy for all religions. Power of doing is infinitely greater than the power of suffering. The power of love is infinitely of greater potency than the power of hatred.

India will be raised not with the power of the flesh, but with the power of the spirit. India will stand not with the flag of destruction, but with the flag of peace, love and cooperation. India will prosper with the garb of *Sannayasin,* not by the power of wealth.

Our ancient mother has awakened once again, sitting on her throne- rejuvenated, more glorious than before.

4

SWAMI VIVEKANANDA ON KARMA-YOGA

The word Karma is derived from the Sanskrit word "Kri" that means to do. All doing action is Karma. Technically,this word also means the effect of actions. In connection which metaphysics, it sometimes means the effects of which our past actions were the causes. But in Karma-Yoga we have simply to do with the word karma as work. The goal of mankind is knowledge that is the one ideal placed before us by Eastern philosophy. Pleasure is not the goal of man, but knowledge is.

All knowledge, secular or spiritual, is in the human mind. In many cases, it is not discovered, but remains covered. We are doing karma all the time. I am talking to you, that is karma. You are listening to me, that is Karma. We breathe, that is karma. We work, Karma. Everything we do physical or mental is Karma. It leaves its mark on us.

Karma in its effect on character is the most tremendous power that man has to deal with. Man, as it werea centre, is attracting all the powers of the universe towards him.

Work is for work sake. There are some who are really the sect of the earth in every country and who work for work's sake, who do not care for name, or fame, or even to go to heaven. They work just because good will come of it. There are others who do good to the poor and help mankind from still higher motives. They believe in doing good. The motives for name and fame seldom bring immediate results. As a rule, they come to us when we are old and have almost done with life. If a man works without any selfish motive in view, does he not gain anything? Yes, he gains the highest. Unselfishness is more paying. It is more paying from the point of view of health also. Love, truth, and unselfishness are not merely moral figures of speech, but they form our highest ideal, because in them lies such a manifestation of power.

Self-restrain is a manifestation of greater power than all outgoing action. A carriage with four horses may rush down a hill unrestrained.

Even a fool may rush the whole world if he works and waits. Let him wait a few years; restrain that foolish idea of governing, and when that idea is wholly gone, he will be a power in the world. The majority of us cannot see beyond a few years. Just as some animals cannot see beyond a few steps. Just a little arrow cycle- that is our world- we have not the patience to look beyond, and thus become immoral and wicked. This is our weakness, our powerlessness.

Even the lowest forms of work are not to be despised. Let the man, who knows no better, work for selfish ends i.e., for name and fame. But everyone should always try to get towards higher and higher motives and to understand them. To work we have the right, but not to the truth thereof. Leave the truth alone. Why care for results? If you wish to help a man, never think what that man's attitude should be towards you. If you want to do a great or good work, do not trouble to think what the results will be.

Intense activity is necessary. We must always work. We cannot live a minute without work. The ideal man is he who, in the minds of the greatest activity, finds the silence and solitude of the desert.

But we have to begin from the beginning to take up the works as they come to us on slowly make ourselves more selfish every day. We must do the work and find out the motive that prompts us. Almost without exception, in the first years, we shall find that our motives are always selfish, but gradually this selfishness will meet by persistence. Then it will come the time when we shall be able to do really unselfish work. We may all hope that same day or other, as we struggle through the paths of life, there will come a time when we shall become perfectly unselfish, all our powers will be concentrated and the knowledge which is ours will be manifested.

THE IDEAL OF KARMA-YOGA

The greatest idea in the religion of the Vedanta is that we may reach the same goal by different paths, and those paths have generalized into four, viz. those of work, love, psychology and knowledge.

Karma-Yoga: Karma-Yoga is a system of ethics and religion intended to attain freedom through unselfishness and by good works. The *Karmayogi* need not believe in any doctrine whatever. He may not believe even in God. He may not ask what his soul is. He may not even think of any metaphysical speculation. He has got his own special aim of realizing selflessness. He has to work it out himself. Every moment of his life must be a realization, because he has to solve by mere work without the help of doctrine or theory.

Raja-Yoga: Raja-Yoga is divided into several steps. The first is *Yama*-non-killing, truthfulness, non-stealing, continence, and non-receiving of any gifts. Next is *Niyama*- cleanliness, contentment, austerity, study and self-surrender to God. Then come *Asana* (posture), *Pranayama* (control of *Prana)*, *pratyahara* (restrain of the senses from their objects) and *Dhyana* (fixing the mind on a spot). *Dhyana* or meditation is a state of super consciousness. The *Yama* and *Niyama* are moral trainings. Without these basic steps no practice of yoga will succeed.

A Yogi must not think or injure anyone by thought, word, or deed. Mercy shall not be for men alone but shall go beyond and embrace the whole world.

Practice is absolutely necessary. You may sit down and listen to me by an hour every day. But if you do not practice, you will not get one step further. It all depends on practice.

This human body is the greatest body in the universe. And a human being is the greatest being. Man is higher than all animals. None is greater than man. Even the Devas (gods) will have to come down again and attain salvation through a human body. Man alone can attain perfection, not even the Devas.

External purification is keeping the body pure. A dirty man will never be a Yogi. There must be internal purification also. That is ordained by the virtues. Of course, internal purity is of greater value than external, but both are necessary. External purity without internal one is of no good.

The theory of Karma is that we suffer from our good or bad deeds. The whole scope of philosophy is to teach the glory of man. All the scriptures sing the glory of man, of the soul. And then in the same breath they preach Karma. A good deed brings such a result and a bad deed such another.

Desires are held together by cause and effect. The past and future exist in their own nature, qualities having different ways.

5

SWAMI VIVEKANANDA ON THE GITA

The Gita is to the Hindus what the New Testament is to the Christians. It is about five thousand years old that happened there a religious celebration of the Hindus in the Battle of Kurukshetra. Swami Vivekananda speaks on the Gita and teaches like this:

The Gita is a great Hindu philosophy. It encompasses the whole humanity with no boundary of religion.

The Vedas are divided into two great divisions- the philosophical and the *Karmakanda* or work portion.

If you know everything, disturb not the childlike faith of the innocent.

Religion is the realization of Spirit as Spirit, not Spirit as matter.

You are Spirit. Realize yourself as Spirit. Do it any way you can.

Religion is a growth; each one must experience it himself.

Everyone thinks- my method is the best. That is so but it is the best for you.

Spirit must stand revealed as spirit.

There never was a time when spirit could be identified with matter.

What is real in nature is the Spirit.

Action is in nature.

In the beginning, there was that Existence. He looked and everything was created.

Everyone works according to his own nature.

You are not bound by law. That is in your nature. The mind is in nature and is bound by law.

If you want to be religious, keep out of religious arguments.

All societies are based on bad generalizations.

A law is that which cannot be broken.

Better never love if that love makes us hate others.

The sign of death is weakness. The sign of life is strength.

What is real in nature is the spirit. The spirit is the life in all action in nature.

It is the spirit that gives nature its reality and power of action.

Action is in nature. The spirit never acts. It merely is, and that is sufficient. It is pure existence, absolute and has no need of action.

All nature is bound by law. The law of its own action; and this law can never be broken. If you could break the law of nature, all nature would come to an end in an instant. There would be no more nature. He who attains freedom breaks the law of nature, and for him, nature fades away and has no more power over him. Each one will break the law but once and forever and that will end his trouble with nature. You are not bound by law. That is in your nature. The mind is in nature and is bound by law.

The moment you form yourself into an organization, you begin to hate everybody outside of that organization. When you join an organization, you are putting bonds upon yourself. You are limiting your own freedom.

If one breaks a law of an order or society, he is hated by the rest.

Spirituality can never be attained until materiality is gone.

The first discourse in the Gita can be taken allegorically.

The Vedas only teach of things in nature, only teach of nature.

We must act beyond emotionalism if we would be able to renounce. Emotions belong to all animals. They are creatures of emotions entirely.

It is not sacrifice of a high order to die for one's young. The animals do that, and just as readily as any human mother ever did. It is no sign of real love to do that; merely blind emotion.

Stay to your soul in regard to vanities, weaknesses, etc. This does not befit thee.

6

SWAMI VIVEKANANDA ON BHAKTI
(NARADA-BHAKTI-SUTRAS)

Bhakti is intense love for God.

It is the nectar of love.

It cannot be used to fill any desire, itself being the check to all desires.

Sannyasa is giving up both- the popular and the scriptural forms of worship.

Sannyasin is the one whose soul goes unto God, and whatever militates against love to God, he rejects.

Giving up all other refuge, he takes refuge in God.

Scriptures are to be followed as long one's life has not become firm. Or else, there is a danger of doing evil in the name of liberty.

When love becomes established, even social forms are given up, except those which are necessary for the preservation of life.

When all thoughts, all words and all deeds are given up unto the Lord, and the least forgetfulness of God makes one intensely miserable, then love begins.

Bhakti is greater than Karma, greater than Jnana, greater than Yoga because *Bhakti* itself is its result, because *Bhakti* is both- the means and the end (fruit).

As a man cannot satisfy his hunger by simple knowledge or sight of food, so a man cannot be satisfied by the knowledge or even the perception of God until love comes. Therefore, love is the highest.

Masters have said about *Bhakti* that:

One who wants this *Bhakti* must give up sense enjoyment, and even the company of bad people.

Day and night, he must think about *Bhakti* and nothing else.

He must go where they sing or talk of God.

The principal cause of *Bhakti* is the mercy of a great soul. Through mercy of God, we get such Gurus.

There is no difference between Him and His ones.

Evil company is always to be shunned.

He who gives up the fruits of work; he who gives up all the work and the Dualism of joy and misery; who gives up even the scriptures, gets that unbroken love for God.

The nature of love is inexpressible. As a dumb man cannot express what he tastes, so a man cannot express his love in words.

Beyond all qualities; all desires, ever increasing, unbroken, the finest perception is love.

When a man gets this love, he sees love everywhere; he hears love everywhere; he talks love everywhere; and he thinks love everywhere.

Bhakti is the easiest way of worship.

Its nature is peace and perfect bliss.

Bhakti never seeks to injure anyone or anything.

Egotism, pride, etc. must be given up.

That love is highest which is concentrated upon God.

When a man loves God so much, his forefathers rejoice; the gods dance; and the earth gets a Master!

To such lovers, there is no difference of caste, sex, knowledge, form, birth or wealth.

Arguments are to be avoided because there is no end to them, and they lead to no satisfactory result.

Giving up all desires of pleasure and pain; gain and loss, worship God day and night. Not a moment is to be spent in vain.

Ahimsa (non-killing), truthfulness, purity, mercy, and godliness are always to be kept.

Giving up all other thoughts- the whole mind should, day and night, worship god. Thus being worshipped day and night, He reveals Himself and makes His worshippers feel Him.

In past, present, and future, love is the greatest!

Nowhere in the world are woman like those of this country. It is the women who are the life and soul of this country. All learning and cultures are centred in them.

Remember these few points:

We are Sannyasins who have given up everything-*Bhakti* and *Mukti*, and enjoyment and all.

To do the highest good to the world, everyone- down to the lowest- is our vow. Welcome *mukti* or hell whichever comes of it.

Ramakrishna Paramahamsa came as the god of the world. Call him a man, or God, or an incarnation just as you please. Accept him each in your own light.

He who will bow before Him will be converted into purest gold that very moment. Go with this message from door to door if you can, my boy, and all your disquietude will be at an end. Never fear. Caring for nothing whatsoever a part of your life is.

A Hindu son never lends to his mother, but a mother has every right over her son and so the son in his mother.

Great undertakings are always fraught with many obstacles. It is these obstacles which knock and shape great characters.

He frees himself from the meshes of his world as a lion from its cage!

The Atman is not accessible to the weak. Hurl yourselves on the world like an avalanche. Let the world crack in twain under your weigh! Hare! Hare! Mahadeva!

One must save the Self by one's own self- by personal prowess.

What makes you weep, my friend? In you is all power. Summon up your all powerful nature, O mighty one, and this whole universe will lie at your feet. It is the Self alone that predominates, and not matter.

To work with undaunted energy! What fear! Who is powerful enough to thwart you?

We shall crush the star to atoms, and unhinge the universe. Do not you know who we are?

One must think of oneself as strong and invulnerable, and so forth.

Arise! Awake! And stop not till the goal is reached.

Life is all expanding; contraction is death. The self-seeking man who is looking after his personal comforts and leading a lazy life- there is no room for him in hell.

Hope is the greatest of miseries. The highest bliss lies in giving up hope.

Hope is the greatest misery. Despair is the greatest happiness.

Collecting fund even for a good work is not good for a Sannyasin.

Seek no help from high or low, from above or below.

Desire nothing and look upon this vanishing panorama as a witness and let it pass.

In wealth is the fear of poverty. In knowledge is the fear of poverty. In beauty is the fear of age. In fame is the fear of backbiters. In success is the fear of jealously. And even in body is the fear of death.

Everything in this earth is fraught with fear. He alone is fearless who has given up everything.

All is for good. All conjunction is for subsequent disjunction. I hope I shall be perfectly able to work alone. The less help from men, the more from the Lord!

Time is short, but the obstacles are many. An organized society is wanted.

The good live for others alone. The wise man should sacrifice himself for others. I can secure my own good only by doing you good. There is no other way, none whatsoever.

Know practically to be the chief cause of all evil. If you show towards anyone more love than towards somebody else, you will be sowing the seeds of future troubles.

If anybody comes to you to speak ill of any of his brothers, refuse to listen to him in toto. It is a great sin to listen even. In that lies the germ of future troubles.

Bear with everyone's shortcomings. Forgive offences by the million. And if you love all unselfishly, all will, by degrees, come to love one another. As soon as they fully understand that the interests of one depends upon those of others; every one of them will give up jealously.

All the Shastras hold that the threefold misery that exists in this world is not natural. Hence, it is removable.

There is no chance for the welfare of the world unless the condition of woman is improved. It is not possible for a bird to fly on only one wing.

No great work can be achieved by humbug. It is through love, a passion for truth, and tremendous energy, that all undertakings are accomplished. Therefore, manifest your manhood.

There is no need to quarrel or disrupt to win anybody. Give your message and leave others to their own thoughts.

Truth alone triumphs, not falsehood.

Religion is not the outcome of the weakness of human nature. Religion is not here because we fear a tyrant. Religion is love- unfolding, expanding, and growing.

All noble undertakings are fraught with obstacles. It is quite in the nature of things. Keep up the deepest mental poise. Take not even the slightest notice of what puerile creatures may be saying against you.

A bit of public demonstration was necessary for Guru.

The doer of good deeds never comes to grief.

Doing good to others (silently) like the spring- this is my religion. I do not want to have any connection with lazy hard-hearted, cruel and selfish men.

If you have the spirit within, you will never fail to attract others. Theosophists' methods can never be ours, for the very simple reason that they are an organized sect.

Individuality is my motto.

No woman shall be allowed to enter any other room except the worship room in the Math. If a woman comes to have a talk with a Sannyasin, she should do it in the visitors Hall.

Better an empty fold than a wicked herd.

Men of evil character shall be rigorously kept out. On no pretense shall their shadow even cross the threshold of my room.

The greatest force is derived from the power of thought. The finer the element, the more powerful it is. The silent power of thought influences people even at a distance, because mind is one as well as many. The universe is a cobweb, minds are spindles.

The soul of man is ever striving after certainty to find something that does not change. It is never satisfied. Wealth, the gratification of ambition or of appetite is all changeable. Once these are attained, man is not content. Religion is the science which teaches us whence to satisfy this longing after the unchangeable.

The philosophy of Vedanta teaches that there are two worlds- the external or sensory, and the internal or subjective.

7

SWAMI VIVEKANANDA'S MANUSCRIPT

An undated and untitled one-page manuscript in Swami Vivekananda's own handwriting extracted from Vol.-IX is reproduced below for general readers of India and abroad:

My nerves act on my brain- the brain sends back a reaction which, in the mental side, is this world.

Something acts on the brain through the nerves, the reaction is this world.

We find that already created outside world (as the result of a previous reaction of the brain) acts on us calling on a further reaction.

Thus inside becomes outside and creates another action, which interior action becomes outside and again acts inside.

The only way of reconciling idealism and realism is to hold that one brain can be affected by the world created as reaction by another brain from inside.

Mind is only a phase of matter.

Man will need a religion so long as he is constituted at present.

The forms will change from time to time.

There were encroachments of a religion on the domains of physical science. Their religion is giving up every day.

A disease does not leave the body by simply repeating the name of the medicine. One must take the medicine. Similarly, liberation does not come by merely saying the word "Brahman". Brahman must be experienced.

Surely, great words do not make a man holy and just; but a virtuous life makes him dear to God.

We feel happy when you are happy. And we suffer when you suffer.

We humbly pray to you- please do not panic due to unfounded fear. Depend upon Lord and calmly try to find the best means to solve the problem. Otherwise, join hands with those who are doing that very thing.

Come. Let us give up this false fear and having faith in the definite compassion of God. Gird up our loins and enter the field of action. Let us give pure and clean lives. Disease, fear of an epidemic, etc. will vanish into thin air by His grace.

Always keep the house and its premises, the rooms, clothes, bed, drain, etc. clean.

Do not eat stale, spoiled foods; take fresh and nutritious food instead. A weak body is more susceptible to disease.

Always keep the mind cheerful.

Everyone will die once. Cowards suffer the pangs of death again and again solely due to the fear in their own minds.

Fear never. Trust not those who earn their livelihood by unethical means, or who causes harm to others. Therefore, at this time when we face the great fear of death, desist from all such behaviour.

During the period of epidemic, abstain from anger and from lust-even if you are householders.

Do not pay any heed to rumours.

Let the wealthy run away! But we are poor; we understand the headache of the poor. The Mother of the Universe is herself the support of the helpless. The Mother is assuring us: Fear not! Fear Not!

Blessed be even all types of Sadhus!

8

EACH IS GREAT IN ITS OWN PLACE

According to the Sankhya philosophy, nature is composed of the three forces called-*Sattva*, *Rajas*, and *Tamas*. These, as manifested in physical world, are what we may call equilibrium, activity and inertness. *Tamas* is typified as darkness or inactivity. *Rajas*is activity expressed as attraction or repulsion. And *Sattva* is the equilibrium of the two.

In every man, there are these three forces. Sometimes, *Tamas* prevails and we become lazy. We cannot move. We are inactive. We are bound down by certain ideas or by mere dullness. At all times activity prevails. In a different man, one of these forces is generally predominant. The characteristics of one man are inactivity, dullness and laziness. The characteristics of those of another man are activity, power and manifestation of energy, and the characteristics of still another man we find arethe sweetness, calmness, and gentleness which are due to the balancing of both action and inaction.

Karma-Yoga has specially to deal with these three factors. By teaching what they are and how to employ them, it helps us to do our work better. Human society is a graded organization. We all know about morality, and we all know about duty. But at the same time, we find that in different countries, the significance of morality varies greatly. What is regarded moral in one country may, in another, be considered perfectly immoral. There must be a universal standard of morality.

Our duty is not to hate ourselves, because to advance, we must have faith in ourselves first and then God. He who has no faith in himself can never have faith in God. Therefore, the only alternative remaining to us is to recognize that duty and morality vary under different circumstances; not that the man who resists evil is doing what is always and in itself wrong.

The *Karmayogi* is the man who understands that the highest ideal is non-resistance and who also knows that this non-resistance is the highest manifestation of powerin actual possession.

Inactivity should be avoided by all means. Activity always means resistance. Resist all evils- mental and physical; and when you have succeeded in resisting, then will calmness comes.

Every man should take up his own ideal and endeavour to accomplish it. That is a surer way of progress than taking up other men's ideals, which he can never hope to accomplish.

All the men and women in anysociety are not of the same mind, capacity or of the same power to do this. They must have different ideals and we have a right to sneer at any ideal. Let everyone do the best he can for realizing his own ideal.

Neither is it right that I should be judged by your standard,nor is it right that you should be judged by my standard. The apple tree should not be judged by the standard of the oak, nor should the oak be judged by that of the apple. To judge the apple tree, you must take the apple standard, and for the oak, its own standard.

Unity in variety is the plan of creation. However, men and women may vary individually. The different individual character and classes of men and women are natural variations increation. Hence, we ought not to judge them by the same standard or put the same ideal before them.

Such a course create only an unnatural struggle, and the result is that a man begins to hate himself, and is hindered from becoming religious and good. Our duty is to encourage everyone in his struggle to live up to his own highest ideal, and strive at the same time to make the ideal as near as possible to the truth.

The Hindu begins his life as a student. Then he marries and becomes a householder in old age. He retires, and lastly he gives up the world and becomes a Sannyasin. To each of these stages of life, certain duties are attached. No one of these stages is intrinsically superior to another.

The life of a married man is quite as great as that of the celibate who has devoted himself to religious work. The scavenger in the street is quite as great and glorious as the king on his throne. It is useless to say that the man who lives out the world is a greater man than he who lives in the world. It is much more difficult to live in the world and worship God than to give it up and live a free and easy life.

The householder should be devoted to God. The knowledge of God should be his goal of life. He must work constantly. He must perform all his duties. He must give up the fruits of his actions to God.

The great duty of the householder is to earn a living. But he must take care that he does not do it by telling lies, or by cheating, or by robbing others, and he must remember that his life is for the services of God, and the poor.

Mother and father are visible representatives of God. The householder, always and by all means, must please them. If the mother and the father are pleased, God is pleased with the man. The child is really a good child who never speaks harsh words to parents.

Before parents one must not utter jokes, must not show restlessness, must not show anger or temper.

Before mother orfather, a child must bow down low, and stand up in their presence, and must not take a seat until they order him to sit. The mother and the father are the causes of this body. So a man must undergo a thousand troubles in order to do good to them.

Even so is his duty to his wife. No man should scold his wife, and he must always maintain her as if she were his own mother. And, even when he is in the greatest difficulties and troubles, he must not show anger to his wife.

He who thinks of another woman besides his wife; if he touches her even with his mind- the man goes to dark hell.

Before woman he must not talk improper language, and never brag of his powers. He must not say, "I have done this, and I have done that."

The householder must always please his wife with money, clothes, inner faith and loving words, and never do anything to disturb her. The man who has succeeded in getting the love of his chaste wife has succeeded in his religion and has all the virtues.

A son should be lovingly reared up to his fourth year. He should be educated till he is sixteen. When he is twenty years of age, he should be employed in some work. He should then be treated affectionately by his father as his equal. Exactly in the same manner,the daughter should be brought up. She also should be educated with the greatest care. And when she marries, her father ought to give her jewels and wealth.

Excessive attachment to food, clothes, and the fondling of the body, and dressing of the hair should be avoided. The householder must be pure in heart and clean is body. He should always be active and ready for work.

To his enemy, the householder must be a hero. Then, he must resist. That is the duty of the householder. He must not sit down in a corner and weep. He must not talk nonsense about non-resistance. If he does not show himself a hero to his enemies, he has not done his duty. And to his friends and relatives, he must be as gentle as a lamb.

It is the duty of the householder not to pay reverence to the wicked,because if he reverences the wicked people of the world, he patronizes wickedness. And it will be a great mistake if he disregards those people who are worthy of respect.

He must not be guessing in his friendship. He must not go out of the way making friends with; and their dealings with other men, reason upon them, and then make friends.

These three things, he must not talk of:

1. He must not talk in public of his fame,

2. He must not preach his own name or his

Own powers, and

3. He must not talk of his wealth, or of anything

that has been told to him privately.

A man must not say- he is poor, or that he is wealthy. He must not brag of his wealth. Let him keep his own courage. This is his religious duty.

The householder is the basis of the whole society. He is the principal earner. The poor, the weak, the children and the women who do not work-all live upon the householder. So, there must be certain duties that he has to perform. And these duties must make him feel strong. He does not make him think that he is doing things beneath his ideal.

If he has done something weak or has made some mistake, he must not say so in public. And if he is engaged in some enterprise and knows he is sure to fail in it must not be expressed. Self-exposure is not only uncalled for, but also unnerves the man and makes him unfit for the performance of his legitimate duties in life.

He must struggle hard to acquire these things- firstly, knowledge; and secondly, wealth. It is his duty. A householder who does not struggle to get wealth is immoral. If he is lazy and content to lead an idle life, he is immoral, because upon him depend hundreds. If he gets riches, hundreds of others will be thereby supported.

Going after wealth is not bad, because that wealth is for distribution. The householder is the centre of life and society. It is worship for him to acquire and spend wealth nobly, for the householder who struggles to become rich by good means and for good purpose goes to heaven.

He must struggle to acquire a good name by all means. He must not gamble. He must not move in the company of the wicked. He must not tell lies. And,he must not be the cause of trouble for others.

The householder must speak with truth and speak gently, using words with people like, which will do good to others. A householder should nottalk of the business of other men.

If a man retires from the world to worship God, he must not think that those who live in the world and work for the good are not worshipping God.

The miseries of the world cannot be cured by physical help only. Until man's nature changes, these physical needs will always arise, and miseries will always be felt and no amount of physical help will pure them completely. The only solution to this problem is to make mankind pure-ignorance of the mother of all evil and all the misery we see.

We may convert every house in the country into a charity asylum. We may fix the land with hospitals but the misery of man will still continue to exist until man's character changes.

We read in the Bhagavad Gita that we must all work incessantly. As work is by nature composed of good and evil, we cannot do any work which will not do some good to somewhere. There cannot be any work which will not cause some harm somewhere.

Every work must necessarily be a mixture of good and evil. We are commanded to work incessantly. Good and evil both will have their results.Both will produce their Karma. Good action will entail upon us good effect and bad action will entail upon us bad effect. But good and bad are both bondage of the soul. The solution given in the Gita in regard to this bondage producing nature of work is that if we do not attach ourselves to the work we do, it will not have binding effect on our soul.

Every act of love brings happiness. There is no act of love which does not bring peace and blessedness as its reaction. Real existence, real knowledge, and real love are eternally connected with one another. True love can never react so as to cause pain either to the lover or to the beloved.

The position of mother is the highest in the world. It is the place in which we learn and exercise the greatest unselfishness. The love of God is the only love that is higher than a mother's love, all others are lower. It is the duty of mother to think of her children first, and thenof herself. Blessed is the man who is able to look upon woman as the representative of the motherland of God. Blessed is the woman to whom a man represents the fatherhood of God.

Blessed are the children who look upon their parents as divinity manifested on the earth. The only way to rise is by doing the duty.

To work properly, you have first to give up the idea of attachment. Secondly, do not mix into fray. Hold yourself as a witness and go on working.

Work incessantly. But give up all attachment to work. Do not identify yourself with anything. Hold your mind free.

Karma-Yoga teaches us that the ordinary idea of duty is the lower duty. We may see that this peculiar sense of duty is very often a great cause of misery. Duty becomes a disease with us if it drags us ever forward. It catches hold of us and makes our whole life miserable. It is the bane of human life. This duty is midday summer sun which scorches the innermost soul of mankind.

9

OTHER VIEWS OF SWAMIJI

Some other views of Swami Vivekananda on different issues are mentioned below:

If you want to be a yogi, you must be free. You must be free from all anxieties. You must please yourself in circumstances where you are alone.

He who desires a comfortable and nice life and at the same time wants to realize the Self is like the fool who, wanting to cross the river, catches hold of a crocodile mistaken it for a log of wood.

The greatest help to spiritual life is meditation (Dhyana). In meditation, we divest ourselves at all material conditions and feel our divine nature. We do not depend on any external help in meditation.

The touch of the soul can point the brightest colour even in the dingiest places. It can cast a fragrance over the vilest thing. It can make the wicked divine.

From time to time, there have been reformers in every religion who stood against all symbols and rituals. But vain has been their opposition, for so long as man will remain as he is. The vast majority will always want something concrete to hold on it. Something which will be the centre of all the thought must form in their minds.

Too much attention to things spiritual disturbs our practical relations in this world.

Man is man so long as he is struggling to rise above nature.

According to the Advaita philosophy, there is only one thing real in the universe which it calls Brahman. Everything else is unreal, manufactured out of Brahman by the power of Maya. To reach back to that Brahman is our goal.

The Atman never comes nor goes. It is never born. Never does it die. It is natural all moving from body to body.

The Hindus believe that creation has come out of the Vedas.

No search has been dearer to the human heart than that which brings to us light from God. No study has taken so much as human energy, whether in times past or present, as the study of the soul, of God, and of human destiny.

Religion is a common sense, every day thing. Nature is conquered by man every day. Man is manifesting his power.

What nation in the world has not ill-treated its women?

The Brahmin is born to worship God. The higher his caste, the greater his social restrictions are. Caste has kept us alive as a nation. While it has many defects, it has much more advantages.

Religion does not consist of pamphlet or book. It consists of looking into the human heart, and finding there the truth of God or immortality.

Religion does not live on bread. It does not dwell in a house.

Meditation is a constant remembrance (of the thing meditated upon) of flowing like an unbroken stream of oil poured out from one vessel to another. When this kind of remembering has been attained (in relation to God), all bondages break.

The test of Ahimsa is absence of jealously. The real lover of mankind is he who is jealous of none.

If Shudras imitate the manners and customs of the Brahmins, they do well. They ought to be encouraged.

Good and bad deeds are not the direct causes in the transformation of nature. But they act as breakers of obstacles to the evolutions of nature, as a farmer breaks the obstacles to the course of water which then runs down by its own nature.

The various religions that exist in the world, although they differ in the form of worship they take, are really one.

God is love personified. He is apparent in everything. Everybody is being drawn to Him whether he knows it or not. When a woman loves her husband, she does not understand that it is the divine in her husbandthat is the great attractive power. The God of Love is the one thing to be worshipped.

Every religion preaches that the essence of all morality is to do good to others.

10

THE PARLIAMENT OF RELIGIONS

In 1892, Swami Vivekananda went to Kanyakumari and spent three days in meditation sitting on the southernmost rock of India. In meditation, India appeared before him in totality. Her past glory, present degeneration, future prospects and his own role in shaping her future—-all became clear to him. He realized that India would survive as she had survived many a time before.

After his meditation is over, he travelled inside India extensively delivering his speeches. Wherever SwamiJi went, he earned much respect for his erudition and conversational power. Many stuck by his talent.

Meanwhile, news came to India that a Parliament of Religions would be held in the United States as part of a celebration to commemorate the four-hundredth anniversary of Columbus's discovery of America. Some suggested that he should go to the West and SwamiJi decided to go to America to attend world ever first Parliament on Religions. Before going to attend, he said his disciples, "The Parliament is being held for this (pointing to himself). My mind says so."

The World Parliament of Religions was held in Chicago on 11th September, 1893. It was a great event in the history of the world. It was a part of world's Columbian exposition. It was held in commemoration of the four-hundredth anniversary of Columbian discovery of America. The Parliament got its publicity. It caught the interest of people the world over. This was the first time that an attempt was made to arrange a dialogue on the religions of the world. Delegation came from all parts of the world. Venue of the Parliament was newly constructed building—-the Art Institute in Chicago.

The objectives of the Parliament were to find common grounds of truth among different religions of the world and to explore what light each religion has afforded to the enrichment of other religions. Such ideas should be welcome at all times, not alone in the context of the Parliament but in the context of the whole humanity. But strangely, the reaction of the Christian community was not completely favourable. To many, the Parliament appeared as an attempt to dishonour Christ by comparing his religion to win others. Archbishop of Canterbury expressed his inability to join Parliament on above ground. To a Minister in Hong Kong, the Parliament was a 'Treason against Christ.'

Though, the organizers were not so sorry in their outlook, the spirit of Christianity worked in their minds. Swamiji did not miss the attitude of the organizers and said later, "The Parliament of Religions was organized with the intension of proving the superiority of Christian religion."

11

SWAMIJI'S ADDRESS AT THE PARLIAMENT

The Parliament opened on 11th September morning, 1893 befitting with a prayer. There was a huge gathering. The solemnity and grandeur of the occasion left no impression on Swamiji. He spoke in the afternoon after four more delegates had spoken. He greeted the audience as "Sisters and Brothers." The whole audience burst out in a peal of applause. And the triumph had taken place even before he actually started his speech.

When the audience calmed down, he made his speech like this: *Yatamatatata Path-* "As many faiths, so many paths." He further said: "It fills my heart with joy unspeakable to rise in response to the warm and cordial welcome which you have given us."

He further went with his speech adding: "I thank you in the name of the most ancient order of monks in the world; I thank you in the name of the mother of religions; and I thank you in the name of millions and millions of Hindu people of all classes and sects..."

Further, he said, "I am proud to belong to a religion which has taught the whole world. We not only believe in universal tolerance, but we accept all religions as true. I am proud to belong to a nation which has sheltered the persecuted and the refugee of all religions and all nations of the earth..."

The present convention, one of the most august assemblies ever held, is, in itself, a declaration to the world of the wonderful doctrine preached in the *Gita*: "Whosoever comes to Me, through whatsoever form, I reach him, all men are struggling through paths, which in the end lead to Me."

Sectarianism, bigotry, fanaticism have long possessed this beautiful earth. They have filled the earth with violence, drenched it with human blood. They have destroyed civilization and sent whole nations to despair. Had they not been, human society would be far more advanced than it is now.

Main points of learning from his Speech are enumerated below:

The Hindu believes that every soul is a circle whose circumference is nowhere, but whose centre is located in the body. He believes that death means the change of this centre from body to body. Not is the soul bound by the condition of matter. In its very essence, it is free, unbounded, holy, pure and perfect.

Hindu is sincere. He does not want to take shelter under sophistry. He is brave enough to face the questions in a manly fashion.

Death means change of centre from one body to another. The present is determined by our past actions, and the future is determined by the present. Soul will go on revolving up or reverting back from birth to birth and death to death.

A man ought to live in this world like a lotus leaf which grows in water but is never moistened by it.

A man ought to live in the world with his heart to God and his hands to work.

It is good to love God for hope of reward in this or the next world. But it is better to love God for love's sake.

The Vedas teach that soul is divine. Man is held in bondage. And the bondage can only fall off through the mercy of God.

Purity is the condition of His mercy.

The Hindu does not want to live upon words and theories. If there are existences beyond the ordinary sensuous existence, he wants to come face to face with them.

The Hindu religion does not consist in struggles.

Science is nothing but the finding of unity. As soon as science would reach perfect unity, it would stop making further progress because it would reach the goal. Religion is the goal of all sciences.

The rose called by any other name would be known by the smell it gives. The tree is known by its fruits. Man is known by his action and good deeds.

Superstition is a great enemy of man. Bigotry is worse.

Idolatry does not mean anything horrible. It is the attempt of mind to grasp high spiritual truth. We can no more think about anything without a mental image. The material image calls up the mental idea and vice-versa. This is why the Hindu uses an external symbol when he worships.

One must not stop anywhere.

External worship is the lowest stage struggling to rise high. Mental prayer is the next stage. The highest stage is when the Lord has been realized.

Unity in variety is the plan of nature.

The whole world of religion is a travelling; upcoming of different men and women through various conditions and circumstances to the same soul.

Every religion is only evolving God out of material and God is the inspirer of all of them.

The Lord has declared to the Hindu in His incarnation as Sri Krishna: "I am in every religion as a thread through a string of pearls. Whenever thou beset extraordinary holiness and extraordinary power rising and purifying humanity, know thou that I am there."

Hinduism means the religion of the Vedas.

In religion, there is no caste. Caste is a social institution. A man from the highest caste as well as a man from the lowest caste may become a monk. I am not a Buddhist and yet I am. We follow the teachings of the Great Master, Lord Buddha. India worships him as God incarnate on the earth.

Buddhist cannot stand without the brain and philosophy of the Brahmins, nor the Brahmins without the heart of the Buddhist.

Separation between the Buddhist and the Brahmins is the cause of the downfall of India. We must avoid it.

Whatever may be the position of philosophy; whatever may be the position of metaphysics; so long as there is such a thing as death in the world; so long as there is such a thing as weakness in the human heart; so long as there is a cry out of the heart of a man in his very weakness, there shall be a faith in God.

If anyone hopes that unity will come by the triumph of any religion and the destruction of the other one; to him I say, "Brothers! Yours is an impossible dream."

Man of each religion must assimilate the spirit of the others and yet preserve his individuality and grow according to his own law of growth.

Upon the banner of every religion will soon be written- "Help and not fight"; "assimilation and not destruction"; "harmony and peace, and not dissension."

God is the source of all beauty and of all sublimity. He is the only object to be loved. Our nature is to love Him and therefore, we love. We do not pray for anything; we do not ask for anything. Let Him place us whatever He likes. We must love Him for love's sake. We cannot trade love.

(All the above points have been extracted from the Speeches delivered by Swami Vivekananda at World Parliament of Religionsheld at Chicago, the USA in September, 1893.)

12

IMPACT OF THE SPEECH

The impact of this lecture was electrifying. Overnight, he became a celebrity. He became the central figure of the Parliament. No success could be more sudden than that of Swami Vivekananda. Indeed, there is hardly anything more startling in the history of oratorical achievements.

Seven thousand people rose to their feet as a tribute to something, they knew not what. The appeal of his simple words of burning sincerity, his great personality, his bright countenance, and his orange robes was so great that next day the newspapers described him as the greatest figure in the Parliament of Religions.

The simple monk with a begging bowl had become the man of hour. An old lady who happened to be present at the Parliament on the first day gave the following account of her experience of listening to Swamiji's first speech: "Well, my lad, if you can resist that onslaught, you are indeed a God!"

The world's Parliament of Religions came to a close. But the people of America could not forget this unique event. They kept talking of it, especially of Swami Vivekananda, the Hero of the Parliament. Streets of Chicago displayed his posters withthe words written—-"The Hindu monk of India." He was followed by hundreds wherever he went. To be near to him or to shake hands with him was considered a privilege. American press andthe intelligentsia were all praise for him. Some described him as a Buddha; some as a Christ and some as a warrior-monk who stood for his country and for the truth we believe in.

Really, he was a great man who could shine in any environment by virtue of his splendid presence, his brilliant conversational power, his magnetic eloquence and above all by his unworldly simplicity and purity of character.

In fact, to know Swami Vivekananda is to like him and to know him well is to revere him. We pay our deep love and high regards to His Holiness Swami Vivekananda, the Spiritual Thunderbolt of India. He has been and really will be a great role-model of Indian youth.